10/03

At the End of Words

At the End of Words

a daughter's memoir

Miriam Stone

CANDLEWICK PRESS
CAMBRIDGE, MASSACHUSETTS

First edition 2003

Library of Congress Cataloging-in-Publication Data

Stone, Miriam R.
At the end of words: a daughter's memoir / Miriam Stone. — 1st ed.
p. cm.
Summary: The author records her feelings and experiences as she realizes that
her mother is dying of cancer.
ISBN 0-7636-1854-3
1. Stone, Martha Kaufman, 1949–1999 — Health — Juvenile literature.
2. Cancer — Patients — Family relationships — Juvenile literature.
3. Mothers and daughters — Juvenile literature.
[1. Stone, Miriam. 2. Stone, Martha Kaufman, 1949–1999. 3. Cancer —
Patients. 4. Mothers and daughters. 5. Youth's writings.] I. Title.
RC265.6.S76 S76   2003
362.1'96994 — dc21   2002073703

2 4 6 8 10 9 7 5 3 1

Printed in the United States of America

This book was typeset in Garamond Ludlow Light.

Candlewick Press
2067 Massachusetts Avenue
Cambridge, Massachusetts 02140

visit us at www.candlewick.com

For my mother,
Martha Kaufman Stone
1949–1999

I will not be divided   from her or from myself
by myths of separation

Adrienne Rich

✸ Fall ✸

September

Reality explodes through my body. I can't feel my fingers, my feet. It hit me hard this time, collapsed me. It's cancer, always cancer. Cancer of the breast, the liver, the lungs. Now the brain. The brain is my mother's most powerful weapon. Everything else slides off of her like layers of dead skin, but her mind drives her through. Who is she without her books, her thoughts, her words? I keep picturing a neon green liquid cancer running through the cracks, the rivers of her brain.

My mind is saturated, but the hammering continues, the truths that happen to other people in other places—tornadoes and hurricanes, news stories, funerals, hospitals. Not me. Not us. I cry ferociously, letting the truth in one breath at a time.

Song

In the quietest morning

air I drive

alone, sliding fog

between my fingers.

I climb to the top

of the parking garage

and sing out

across the intersection

because

nobody can hear.

October

7:30 A.M. I tumble from bed, slide into jeans, roll over the waist. Flip my head and draw a tight ponytail. Grab a sweater, jacket, a granola bar from the kitchen. I'm late already. The halls at school are swarming with people. Kids in black marshmallow jackets stuff themselves through the door three at a time, fall air fastened to their clothing, the crunching of leaves on their feet.

Movie in first period English. Everyone is half-asleep. I try to focus on the screen but I see nothing, just images and colors flickering across the room, empty noises bouncing off the walls. In my mind I see hundreds of snapshots. My mother on the skating rink. Click. My mother on a hospital bed, smiling at me with her thin mouth. Click. Me crawling onto the couch beside her with the newest J. Crew catalog, ordering shirts for her in medium, even though she's less than a small, so no one can see the outline of bandages and tubes on her chest. Sweaters that zip up from the front so she can take them off quickly in case of a hot flash. And, of course, a T-shirt for me, as my commission for being her personal shopping consultant.

Yesterday I came home from school and found her on the couch as usual. She was still in pajamas, a blanket draped over her legs, the TV tuned to a talk show that she wouldn't have stood for a year ago yet now watched with mild enthusiasm. "Hey, Mom," I said as I walked in. She looked up abruptly, broke into a smile.

"Hi, sweetheart." She gazed at me. "You can turn this off." I plopped down across from her in the big brown chair. She was still smiling. "Did you get that English paper back yet?" she asked.

"Yep," I said. "I got a B-plus."

"That's *very* good." She nodded her head in approval. She had edited it the night before I turned it in, but had made hardly any corrections. Usually there were pencil markings everywhere — two lines under letters to be capitalized, a question mark by a misspelled word. Lately my work was left almost untouched by her meticulous hand.

"Guess what happened today?" I began. I proceeded to tell her about the latest drama between my friend Jessica and her homecoming date, what I was thinking of wearing, what outrageous thing my Spanish teacher had said in class . . . and so on and so forth to the nodding of her head, her glasses catching the light up and down, up and down. After a while she didn't nod anymore. She stared at the blank TV screen. I gabbed on, barely noticing.

She stopped me. "Miriam, I'm tired."

"Okay," I said, slightly hurt that she didn't care to hear the end of the story. "Well, I need to go work on my applications." I heaved myself out of the deep chair.

"Good," she replied, her eyes closed, her breathing already heavy and slow. I paused at the doorway to watch her tiny body rise and fall under the blanket. *It's amazing how thin she is,* I thought. Her thick glasses make bug-eyes on her face. Her wrists look ready to crack and fall off. The chemo triggered osteoporosis, drank away any muscle on her bones. She is a body of breakable pieces, a small china cup, a glass figurine.

In class, it's this image of her that floats around my brain. *She's withering away,* I think. *I wonder how long it will be.* I feel myself begin to cry. I shut my eyes quickly and tightly. *Shut up!* I scream at myself from inside. *What are you saying? Nobody else thinks she's going to die, not Dad, not David, not her own mother, Jojo. It's just the chemo that makes her this way. If you think she's going to die, everyone will think you've given up. She'll think you've given up.*

"Naptime's over," says the teacher. I open my eyes. The movie is over. The teacher turns on the lights. The bell rings and we shuffle into the crowded hall.

"Are you okay?" a friend asks in passing.

"I'm fine," I say, and try to force a smile.

5

·   ·   ·

In late afternoon sun, we smoke bowls on plastic patio chairs in my friend's backyard. I breathe in, letting the smoke wander through me. We laugh and raid the kitchen, watch stupid television until it's time to go home for dinner.

Dad thinks I should stay home more; there's so much to do around the house. And then there's Mom, of course, alone in the den in her pajamas. I want to go home. That nagging feeling, the dread that this may be the last time I have to spend with her, never really goes away. But spending extra time doesn't feel right either. I am supposed to be strong with her, fight with her. If she sees that I am trying harder, asking questions about her life, telling her strange and intimate things, she'll know that I've given up, that I've stopped fighting, that my hope is gone.

I come home at 7:00 as I am coming down from my high. Mom goes to sleep soon after and I sit on the rug in my room upstairs. I write long, furious poems, the words trailing off along the edges. I used to write until I could put a finger on my feelings, categorize and label, solve the problem, move on. But moments of clarity like that never come anymore. Muddled poems remain untailored in notebooks. Disjointed lines sprawl across yellow legal pads. Tonight I fall asleep with the paper in my hands, the pen bleeding ink into the comforter.

Dreaming of My Period

I wake to blood on my underwear, stained
sheets, knotted stomach, full breasts,
curled into a ball, my body pulls
to the window, the dull,
gray-gold light on the sill,
this moon over this body,
this body in dream.

You sleep a room from me,
body abandoned
by your period, one breast left,
your pale head shivers
under thin scarves.
Your frail, sexless body,
womanhood stripped piece by piece.
No longer attached to the moon,
you are left dangling,
waiting to be swept
away by the breeze.

November

This weekend we take a campus tour. Just Mom, Dad, a tour guide, a wheelchair, and me. I clumsily push her along brick walkways and uneven sidewalks in the freezing gray air. She is wearing her huge fur coat, her tiny head protruding like a turtle's, her hands placed pleasantly on her lap as she nods approvingly at the size of the dorm rooms, the dark wood dining hall, the cavernous library.

"And the flight home is so short." She smiles. "You'll be able to come back for weekends, if you want."

As Dad struggles to put the wheelchair in the trunk of a cab, I stand on the sidewalk to take one last look. I feel her gaze on me through the window. She never should have traveled with us. She is way too weak. But she had insisted on coming in her quiet, unquestionable way. I turn back toward the street and catch her eye. I haven't been accepted to school yet. She hasn't announced her death yet. But in that glance is our first goodbye.

Back at the high school the tightness in my chest is suffocating. I slip into my guidance counselor's office. Before I know it, I'm crying and shaking and saying things I didn't even know I felt. "Everything is catching up with me," I say. "Everyone has the same stuff to deal with, SATs and applications and everything. But I just feel like I can't handle it anymore. I can't do my work. I'm so tired all the time. I'm not sure what else to do." I've already quit volleyball. It was such a relief, that letter to the coaches, that quick flick of the pen. *My mother is very sick and I need to spend more time at home. I will not be completing the rest of the season with the team.* Why did I even tell them my mother was sick? I've hardly even been spending more time at home. Am I using her sickness as an excuse?

My counselor asks if I want him to tell my teachers about my mother. Maybe they'd give me some breaks — they'd be more understanding. No, I shake my head. That's okay. I just need to step up to things. It's my own fault for slacking off. My mom has been sick since I was in eighth grade. I have always managed to stay in control. But he remains unconvinced. He's going to talk to my teachers, and my brother David's too. At least I won't have to say it to anyone's face.

I leave his office ashamed, angry, stifled with guilt.

How did this all happen, the crying, the pity? Maybe I like people feeling sorry for me. Maybe I'm the kind of person who takes the easy way out. While my mother is sick at home, I'm here sliding by on her pain, using her.

I want to go home, fess up and tell her everything. Instead I cut class and stand with friends, stamping feet near the tennis courts, hands stuffed in our coat pockets. Cigarette smoke melds with our freezing breath into tiny white clouds above our heads.

Blueprint

Stories like loose nails jut out

from your structure —

French rock stars, hippie boyfriends, the Beatles in Paris.

St. John's in the '60s: Homer and Aristotle,

an anorexic roommate, the Maryland air.

The day you told me about the first time you had sex

we were driving to your mother's in the blue van.

Parked outside, keys stripped

from the ignition, casually, in conversation,

like it was something we discussed every day.

I wondered if your mother told you

the things that you tell me.

Now I hoard your stories, scavenge

for your words like water. I want the glue that holds you

together. I need the architecture, the angles

of your inside.

I want to ask: what does love smell like,

what color sky makes your skin melt,

what does death taste like,

and are you afraid?

❦ Winter ❦

December

Standing barefoot in the bathroom in jeans and a bra, I stare at the mirror with rough distaste. I lean in to inspect my sunken eyes, the purple, wrinkled skin beneath them. The black pupils grow in radius as I stare. It is painful to keep my eyes open these days. I go to sleep late and wake up late, wearing the same clothes to school that I've slept in, and never brush my hair.

I run my fingers through the greasy, rough strands. I have never looked or felt so separate from my body. I imagine my self balled up in some dark corner of my frame, perhaps shoved between two ribs or lodged behind my stomach.

From beneath a pile of papers in my room I dig up an old pair of scissors. Back at the mirror, I grab a large lock of hair and begin to cut. The delicious sound of slicing fills the air. Blond locks drop dramatically into the sink, onto the floor, catching on my stomach, my jeans. I can't stop cutting. I don't even look in the mirror anymore. What started as an inch now turns to two and three and four and suddenly I have hair to my ears. I toss the scissors into the sink and run my fingers through, from my forehead to the back of my neck. I turn my head left, then right, inspecting the new me. I feel light, free, and beautiful for the first time in months. I run downstairs to show Mom.

I spend Friday night at an old friend's house, surrounded by warm faces, laughter soaked with memories. The phone rings. It's my father.

"Mom's in pain again," he says. "She's been moaning for an hour. She can't speak. We don't know what it is. The nurse is coming. We may have to go to the hospital." I hang up the phone, my hand trembling, make my apologies, and scramble into the car to drive home.

Pain

She is stuffed

beneath blankets, head pressing

down pillows, back arched,

teeth clenched, while the walls,

the windows, the rest of us

wrap around her

low and lonesome moaning,

her unimaginable universe.

January

Today we decided to stop treatment. We were in the hospital, in the same unit we had been in four years ago, when Mom had a bone marrow transplant. Things were so different then. I remember visiting her after lacrosse practice, sweaty and hungry, brimming with stories. Today I sat biting my nails in a chair, knees curled up to my chest. Today was the official beginning of the end. Mom will be moved to a hospice, where people wait to die.

David, Dad, and I are sitting at the kitchen table, speaking slowly. We talk about how it feels to give up, like when you let go of a rope you've been gripping for hours and your muscles are molded into holding on, like clay. We watch our images in the large window — our mirror selves superimposed on the dark outlines of trees. It strikes me that this is my family now. A father and children. Two men and me.

Not so long ago the four of us were sitting at this table together, eating dinner, and David said something and Mom said something back and it didn't make any sense and David rolled his eyes and I laughed and Mom shook her head, saying, *I don't know where my mind is.* David and I would get annoyed at her often, and then we'd catch ourselves and feel ourselves breaking inside because we were so angry. We were angry at our mother for disappearing on us. Angry at her for making less and less sense. Angry at the chemo for blurring her thoughts and her eyes and for clogging up her ears. Angry at her for not reading books like she used to, for ordering things from the home shopping channel and having the nerve to say the home shopping channel was "nice." Angry because some days we could barely recognize her. Angry because we couldn't tell what angered us the most — her or the cancer or her brain or the chemo or ourselves for even being angry at all.

So we'd close our eyes and pray that she hadn't noticed our annoyance, but of course she'd noticed and it broke her too because she knew she'd changed and her body was disappearing and her mind was too. And that is painful enough but unbearable when your children know it and when your children are angry at you for what is not your fault and everybody cannot move and cannot talk. My family was paralyzed and we were breaking apart but we kept gripping until our fingers went numb because we could not — we would not — admit defeat.

Now we say it. She is going to die. A month at most, the doctors say. And in the ripping and tearing of that one decision everything we have been holding together falls away. And here we are at this table where we've been so many nights before, but now we just talk and breathe and stare at our reflections in the window. We are surprised when our fingers tingle as the feeling comes back into them and the anger is washed over by relief. And the relief is swirling with sadness. We lean back into the tall kitchen chairs and absorb the force of what is to come.

February

The hospice smells like cleaning fluid and stuffy rooms. Outside the snow is melting. Lake Erie licks the shore. Everything is smeared with an ice blue. Next to the bed there is a little stereo that we can play Ella on. Sometimes at 5:30 we watch *The Simpsons* on the television. But mostly we just sit with her. People visit and read her favorite passages — E. B. White, Nabokov, the Bible. I read her Robert Frost, though I've never liked him much.

Nurses come in to change her or fix a tube or do mysterious things to her body that I know I don't want to see, so I go down the hall and visit the little old lady who gives me chocolates from her son. She smells of cigarettes after lunch and dinner. Her room is cluttered with flowers and cards. Mom's room isn't decorated.

I go to school when I can drag myself out of bed. Every day at 4:00 David and I climb in the Jeep and take Route 90 to the hospice. He smokes little cigars through the crack in the window, the cold air battling with the heaters. I force him to listen to Ani DiFranco on the tape player. We don't talk.

I pace the hospice halls in socks. I play my music on the piano in the center of the building, where the halls stem off like spider legs and the notes spill down the hallways. They almost reach Mom's room. She doesn't talk or move anymore. She just breathes in and out steadily with her mouth open. Her skin is pale and her eyes glazed and I sometimes imagine her a beached whale, pulling in her last breaths on an unfamiliar shore.

Tonight we stay in her room until 7:00. Dad takes us to his favorite brewpub, where we sample beer in little glasses and eat hamburgers. As we are finishing, a nurse calls Dad on his cell phone. She says it will be soon. Tonight, tomorrow, next week. We drive back to the hospice in silence.

I kneel by her bed. I have been left alone to "say goodbye" while Dad, David, and Jojo are in the hallway. I stare at her and wonder if I will say the right thing, if there is a right thing, and if she can even hear me. All this time I've been waiting for the right moment to tell her everything, and when it's here I have no idea what to say. I want to open my mouth and pour out poetry, but instead the words topple, released from a cluttered closet.

I begin to tell her about love and womanhood and individuality, and everything she has made me I spew back to her like in grade school like I am five again and I will not talk to strangers and I will look both ways and I will tell you where I am going and what I am feeling and I will not let anyone dictate who I am or should be and I will not open myself for people who don't deserve me and I will follow what I love to be and do and see and I will have passion but not be ruled by it and I will hold on to what I know is true no matter what and I will fight for it and speak my mind and I will value people and love and friendship and laughter above all above all above all and I will go out and do great things because of you and for you and I know you'll be with me and I will never ever forget you ever and I will never love you any less. Not for one day. Not for one minute. You will be with me as much fifty years from now as you are today.

At the end of words there is only her breathing. I put my head on her arm and cry to the rhythm, our symphony of goodbyes.

In Between Breaths

Hour over

hour

I watch her rise

and fall.

In between breaths,

the room throbs.

My fingers scream.

I wait for her white

cheeks to move.

My heart stops.

I stare until

the breathing breaks.

I sleep beside her,

curled in jeans on the floor,

yellow morning

spreads over me.

Voices circle,

pale nurses swarm,

I hear only my own breath.

Elegy Written for My Mother
As read at her funeral, March 4, 1999

Mellow guitar floats through the air

like an aroma,

the flames of the candle stretch

skyward.

I huddle under my down comforter

and feel its weight sink onto me

like the weight of each day

I wake   aching,

deflated,

wishing for night's cool fingers

to soothe me

back to sleep,

instead feeling the hot

breath of dawn

on my neck,

my alarm clock cackling.

But you take each morning

like a holiday.

You rise to the occasion,

you sip your morning coffee

in your bathrobe

and flash your lightning smile.

We drag our feet to the door.

I envy your love of waking.

Car headlights

cut through cool fog at rush hour —

life to you —

the scent of coffee brewing

and the swishing of the plastic

off the morning paper

chant

fight   fight   fight.

The day stretches and pulls you
but you   never   break.
Light, life, love,
strength, the will to live
enhanced at each dawn.

Nighttime creeps in.
I plead for sleep so I can escape.
You sleep dutifully,
resting the forces,
rearm   reorganize   reunite
prepare for tomorrow's breaking of light
over the horizon
like a child being born.

You didn't just battle
to gain a little more,
you exploded with strength
and went to war.

❧ Spring ❧

March

3:05 P.M. The building breathes in, stretches its fingers, and exhales. Students explode from every doorway, bursting like sun rays into the afternoon. Frisbees fly, car stereos thump, laughter dangles from the naked trees. I walk to the car at just the right pace, climb in, and roll down the windows. Lenny Kravitz in the CD player. Nice. The trees wrap the road like a canopy. Ducks litter our small lake. I had forgotten how beautiful this town is. It's exhilarating just to drive through it in the sunlight.

I couldn't have felt something like this a year ago. Never before have I appreciated what it means to be alive on a day like today, to be so acutely aware of the absence of pain. It is a dive into cool water, a flood of light after days of rain. I feel okay today, and someday, I imagine, I'll feel okay every day. For now I just drive home, singing at the top of my lungs, feeling light and free for the first time in months.

Your Presence

Your presence still
fills the house like warm
air. We've tried to

empty the rooms of you,
we've sorted and claimed
and stored, but

your shoes still tap
inside the storage room,
your wedding dress hums,

packaged in your perfume,
and yesterday I thought I
saw you in the mirror,

sometimes your voice creeps

up through the vents and I can

feel you tingling

on my skin like today

you told me you loved me but

it's been weeks

since I've seen you

and weeks from now I still

won't see you and I wake

to the word "never"

in the mornings, clinging

like moisture to the air.

April

"Do you think you'll find out today?" my friend Jessica asks as we pull into the driveway. It is past the day they said the letters would come. After being deferred from early decision in the fall and after receiving letters from everywhere else I'd applied to, I'd pretty much had it with this school.

"Who knows," I say as I step onto the driveway. "I could care less what they tell me, ya know? I mean, I don't think I'm even going to go there. I just want them to send the stupid letter already." I stride across the concrete to the front door, casually stopping to bend over the wicker mail basket. A familiar nervousness twists in my stomach. Bills, ads, magazines. No letter. Disgusted, I leave the mail for someone else to bring in. We walk in through the garage door.

Inside, I pace the kitchen. "I don't understand why it's not here yet," I say. "Everyone else has heard from them. It just doesn't make sense. You know, I'm just going to check again. Maybe I missed it or something."

I walk through the hall to the front door. As I open it a large FedEx envelope resting on the storm door falls at my feet. My heart jumps and my fingers numb. I slide down the wall and pick the envelope up slowly. I peel away the layers to the large blue folder. I stare at it and I can't believe it's real and sitting in front of me. After all this time.

Jessica and I burst outside and jump in the car to go celebrate. Turning onto the street, I still can't process what has just happened. I can barely feel the steering wheel. The traffic filters by around me. I feel like I'm floating. Then it hits me. *She doesn't know.* I swerve to avoid a turning car. *I can't tell her. She doesn't know.* The car is suffocating. I can't breathe. Cars scream by.

"Pull over!" calls Jessica from worlds away. Breathless, I turn onto a side street and crumple over the steering wheel. Jessica places her hand on my shaking back.

"I just wish I could have told her," I say between gasps. "I wanted her to know where I'm going. I just wanted her to know I'd be okay."

"She knows," says Jessica calmly. "She always believed you'd get in. And she *always* knew you'd be okay."

"I know," I say. "I know that she knew. I just wish I could tell her. God, I just wish I could tell her." I exhale slowly, turn around, and drive home. I call my father at work. "Dad? I got in."

For a Walk with My Grandmother

Jojo and I walk

on the sidewalk together,

she ahead of me.

She sits down to rest.

I wait as she blots her eyes,

her walnut-shell skin.

How long will we wait?

I have no one to follow,

you no one to lead.

We have to go on.

Let us leave a space between

your footsteps and mine.

She'll float over us.

As a pyramid we'll walk.

Mothers and daughters.

May

At a trendy hair salon the afternoon before prom, Jessica and I sit beside each other, mirrors framing her thick, dark waves, my blond hair trim and neat against my face. Jessica's mother waits patiently behind us. I watch as she observes her daughter, her concerned eye and slightly nagging voice, and wonder what it would be like to have my own mother standing behind me right now. It's hard to imagine, now that I have taken on my independence like a call to war. I am fiercely solo these days, taking any sort of help or advice as an offense. I cringe when I see a mother involved in her children's lives in any way, from reminding them about a dentist's appointment to hugging them when they leave the house.

"What do you think about curling these ends here?" asks my perky hairdresser, waving her weapon of choice menacingly above my head.

"Um, okay," I say as I sit back and let her loose on my hair. Mom would have liked this. She didn't even go to her senior prom, but she loved getting dressed up, doing girlie things. We did our share of shopping and watching *My So-Called Life* together. *I'm going to miss that,* I think as Jessica's mom takes a step back to admire her daughter, her own dark curls looking fuller in the salon lighting.

I glance back at the mirror. I imagine my mother behind me, nodding her head with approval, her neck long and thin like mine, telling me I look beautiful, how proud she is of me, and hugging me as I walk out the door.

Summer

June

It's almost midnight when I hear the garage door open. I'm sitting in the computer room in Dad's big black chair. I feel minuscule compared to the cushion around me, like a queen in her throne. I hear Dad's unmistakable cough in the kitchen, the one I heard from the stage during band concerts, the one I heard on the radio when he and Mom went to see Garrison Keillor, the one assuring me that someone else is still up when I can't fall asleep. Soon I hear his footsteps on the stairs and the hinges of the door swinging open. He walks in and sits beside me, still in his gray sweatsuit from volleyball. We chat about the volleyball game, the usual crowd of players, the traditional after-game beer at Brennan's Pub.

"You know, Miriam," he says, "some of my volleyball friends are trying to set me up with people." I look at him abruptly.

"What do you mean?"

"Well, one of the women in the group kept talking to me tonight about this friend she has. But I don't know. I don't think I'm ready to date just yet."

Date? I think. *My dad's going to date?* It had never occurred to me before this. Somehow I had always pictured my dad growing old by himself, moving to a smaller house when we were gone, maybe traveling the world after he'd retired. But not *dating.* Not finding anyone else. Dad didn't have a life outside of Mom. She was his soul mate. What would be the point of looking for someone else?

"So what did you tell her?" I ask carefully.

"I just told her not right now. But you know, I'll have to start sometime. People have been asking. It seems like everyone's got a friend they want me to meet. There are a lot of single middle-aged women out there." I try to let the words sink in. I can't believe what I'm hearing. "What do you think, Miriam? I mean, how would you feel if I started to date?"

"Ummm . . ." I don't know what to say to him. What would Mom think? What would she want me to say? "Well, I don't know. It would be weird, I guess. I haven't really ever thought about it. What did . . . Did you ever talk to Mom about it?"

He pauses and twirls his hair between his fingers. "Mom mentioned it once," he says softly. "She said she knew eventually I would find someone else, and that didn't bother her. But she said she never wanted to talk about it again." He looks at his reflection in the dark window.

"Well, I . . . I guess it would be okay. I mean, it'll just take some getting used to," I say with more conviction than I feel.

"Yeah. We all have a lot to get used to. Well," he says as he pulls himself to his feet, "I'm going to bed. Good night." He kisses my forehead.

"Good night," I reply with a smile.

For Dad

I

Your porcupine beard scratched

when you kissed my cheek good night, you hugged

my frame too hard and my collarbone hurt.

I never told you. I loved the whistling

Of your breath from your nose, I loved your soft

graying curls, how you twirled them with your fingers,

leaning back in your black chair, thinking.

Each night I slept to your gentle tapping on the keyboard.

II

We worked late into the night:

me on my carpet, surrounded by textbooks like wings,

you down the hall, illuminated in blue from the screen,

your cough the oldest lullaby.

When it was the worst you'd carry her to the bathroom.

You didn't sleep or go to work or do anything

but count out her pills, make sure she was warm,

talk to doctors on the phone, hold her hand while she slept.

III

We rebuild ourselves from nothing, this time,

remembering to glue each other in —

hands, feet, hair, eyes.

She used to say how alike we were,

I didn't believe her. I find myself breaking

into your sentences now. It drives

you crazy, but sometimes, you let me

finish your thought.

July

Today is my eighteenth birthday. I wake up to find a tan, crinkled envelope on my nightstand. A Post-It note on top reads "Miriam — I found this in some of Mom's things. Happy birthday. Love, Dad." In the center of the envelope is written "Miriam Rachel Stone" in my mother's handwriting, and in the bottom right corner, "On her eighteenth birthday." I open the envelope greedily, my eyes still hazy with sleep and disbelief.

My dearest Miriam,

I write this on your first birthday in the hope that when you are grown to be a young woman, it may help you to understand me. I can't tell how our lives will be then, but this letter is to explain how it began.

When you were born and I saw your beautiful little face as you looked solemnly at your father, I felt a tremendous new love. That love is as strong now as a year ago, and it grows every day. You wouldn't think that a baby could teach, but I have learned from you that I have a capacity to love that keeps increasing. It's a wonderful feeling. I see it in your father's eyes when he looks at you, too.

You have also taught me to look at the world in a new way. As you have grown this year, each accomplishment has been a triumph for us both. Every door for you is a challenge; every step is a mountain that you conquer. When I see your determined look, I try to let you do it yourself because you are so pleased when you win.

You have taught me patience. The beginning of your life meant that I had to work hard to nurse you. I was rewarded by seeing you grow fatter and happier every day. Rocking you in the middle of the night and singing old songs to you was the most peaceful feeling.

Now that you are growing old and becoming independent as a one-year-old I see your own nature coming through. You are a little stubborn but very sweet-tempered, with a smile for everyone. Your laugh is wonderful to hear, and when you cry, it breaks my heart.

This year has been the first for you. It has been the most happy for me. When you read this, I want you to know that my greatest wish is to return the happiness you have given me and my hope is that you will know as much love each day as I feel for you today.

Your mother

On Being Here

My head is on his chest,
and I am contemplating
the paint on his hands,
small white flecks
speckled across his palms. *This is me,*
existing, without her.

I used to talk to her, I felt her
in the room with me, in the void
between sleep and waking I could swear
she was still alive.

But in the golf-course lamplight, in August
evening mist, she is
absence, and I am
slightly damp and shivering,
his body beneath me rising
and sinking again back to the earth.

I dream of coming home to the dark brick house we used to live in, with the swing set in the back and the pachysandra in the front and the Tierneys next door with their yard sales every year, where I was a clown for Halloween and David was Ringo at the block party and I always walked to school down Demington and waited for Lynne while she took her vitamins, and then I came home and did errands with Mom and in the fall at Jojo's we'd jump in the leaves and in the winter we'd pray for school to be closed, and in the spring the puddles and in the summer the sun and on 2193 Chatfield it was always just like that, the same every year.

But in my dream I am standing in the front yard with Mom. She is skinny and pale like she was just before she died, and she tells me she's gotten out of the hospital. She says she's recovered from the cancer and is home trying to regain her strength. But I've been away at school this whole time and I thought that she was dead, and that's why I haven't called and that's why I haven't been to visit her. Well, she says, it's lucky that I am home now to see that she is still alive. Now I can sit down and tell her all the things I've been meaning to, like I got an A on a term paper, and I read all the Great Books and we should discuss them, and I had sex for the first time and it was wonderful. Now we can be mother and daughter again, and I can have someone to tell everything to. Things will be just as they were then, as they should be.

But it can't be the same, I tell her. We aren't really our family anymore because I am gone and David's curls have gone straight and Dad has a girlfriend who he really likes, and I ask her how she feels about that and she shrugs her shoulders as if to say, It's not great, but what can you do?

So instead we just walk down the street together so that she can build up strength in her legs, and she is faster than I am as always, her powerful strides leaving me trotting two steps behind. Then we reach the part where the road curves around the oak trees and I see that she is wearing ice skates. I know I can't keep up with her as she skates away around the corner, so I stop and watch her figure growing smaller and smaller. I just stand there staring until she is gone and I wake up.

September 1, 1999

Dear Mom,

I am leaving for college tomorrow. I am leaving home and our family and the place I was born and where you were born and where you died. I am leaving and there is so much to say. I say things out loud to you sometimes, like that night on the porch, when it was March and freezing, and I was talking to the sky, surprised that it did not respond. But this time I am writing it all down, fighting impermanence with permanence. I know that if I write it you will read it, and neither of us will forget what was said.

There were things I told you that you already knew. I told you all the time that I'd be okay. I told you at your bedside. I told the sky that night on the porch. I still tell you when I'm lying in my bed at night. Mom, you know I'll be okay, I say. I'll leave home and I'll go to school and I'll do things, amazing things, and

I'll do them for you because you made me who I am. I promised you these things, as if you ever doubted them. I told you that I loved you. You knew that too.

There were things I didn't tell you, things we never spoke about. Like how your death hollowed me out inside. That seeing you lying there, that watching you die, was like watching my past and future, things I had always taken for granted, you at my graduation, my wedding, as a grandmother, as my best friend, watching these things grow thin and die too. We never talked about death out loud. Just once, when I was lying in bed with you, and I just cried. We just cried. There were so many things we both knew but did not say. Death comes, and everything around it, whether you acknowledge it or not.

But there are certain things you don't know, things that should be said. Like how beautiful your death was. How simple, on top of its intricacies. Your decline poetic, your fight heroic, the love that poured from you and to you so astounding, it swelled even the room you died in. It still billows in me every time I breathe. Your death gave as much life as it destroyed. It marked my passage into my new life, equipped with the strength of a mother and daughter wrapped in one. It gave me love without boundaries.

And your death brought me poetry, an abundance of it. More words and poetry than I'll ever squeeze into one poem or one book or a lifetime of books. It is the ability to write of the echo in Jojo's sadness, her beautiful, clear, mother tears soaring from her eyes, buried deep in her skin. To notice how David and I hugged in the hallway outside your room the night before you died, and cried in front of each other for the first time. To understand how the beauty and love you gave Dad in one life left him open and ready to the same sort of love in a new life.

Your death, though only the smallest part of you, was a part of you, and so I accept your death and what it brought even as I celebrate your life. As I love you every moment of every day. As that love propels me through everything I do. I live as a memorial to you.

Your daughter,
Miriam